■SCHOLASTIC

Funny Read-Aloud Plays
with LEVELED PARTS

12 Reproducible, High-Interest Plays
That Help Students at Different Reading Levels Build Fluency

Justin McCory Martin

NEW YORK • TORONTO • LONDON • AUCKLAND • SYDNEY
MEXICO CITY • NEW DELHI • HONG KONG • BUENOS AIRES

Teaching *Resources*

Editor: Mela Ottaiano
Cover and interior design: Jason Robinson
Interior illustrations: Terry Sirrel

ISBN-13: 978-0-439-87027-6
ISBN-10: 0-439-87027-5

Contents

Introduction

Welcome to *Funny Read-Aloud Plays With Leveled Parts*. The aim of this book is to get kids jazzed about reading aloud so they can build fluency. Inside, you'll find 12 plays with dialogue for different characters written at two levels of reading difficulty. Chances are, the students in your class vary in their reading proficiency. With these plays, all your readers will be able to participate together. Even your most reluctant readers are likely to be motivated to "perform" in these highly engaging plays.

This book is divided into four sections: Cliffhangers, Mysteries, Spooky Stuff, and Just for Laughs. These categories are specifically chosen to appeal to your students. They'll read about a talking pizza, superheroes, and a french fry eating contest, a scary story told from the monsters' point of view, and more.

Each play features about eight characters. The dialogue for half of the characters rates between 2.0 and 3.9 on the Spache Readability Index. (Spache is a respected and widely used method for measuring the relative difficulty of passages.) For the other characters, the text rates between 4.0 and 5.9. But you won't necessarily be able to tell which characters are at what level. More important, neither will your students. This is by design. In a given play, a Level 1 character (2.0 to 3.9 on the Spache index) might get a long stretch of dialogue, while a Level 2 character (4.0 to 5.9) might get a shorter piece but with more challenging vocabulary words. A key at the back of the book will help you discretely match characters to students' reading levels. This way, all students will be able to read their parts comfortably and, in the process, build their confidence and fluency. Everyone will benefit from this shared experience.

Building Fluency With Read-Aloud Plays

As you may know, fluency is an important aspect of reading. When a student can read text quickly and accurately with meaning and expression, she can be said to read fluently. But fluent reading is not just about speed; it's also about understanding and interpreting the text. It's about comprehension. When a reader is struggling to sound out words and reads haltingly, he cannot pay attention to the meaning of the text and so cannot comprehend what the text is about. A fluent reader, on the other hand, can focus on the meaning because he is not bogged down by the features of print.

How can students build fluency? Research shows that repeated reading helps improve word recognition, speed, and phrasal reading—all keys to fluent reading. As with any skill, repeated practice leads to proficiency. So, for students to develop fluency, they need to read a lot!

That's where these read-aloud plays come in. Students want to perform well, so they're motivated to practice reading their parts over and over again until they can read their lines fluently and with comprehension. To sum up, these plays give students an authentic reason to develop their fluency and comprehension skills through repeated reading.

How to Use the Plays

Divide the class into groups according to the number of characters in the play. You may decide to have different groups of students working on different plays, or have all the groups work on the same play. Make sure you have an equal number of at- or above-level readers and below-level readers in the group. Assign each student a role based on his or her reading level. (Refer to the key on page 64 to help you match characters to students' reading levels.) Then photocopy the plays and distribute copies to students.

Try the following steps to make the best use of the read-aloud plays:

1. Model fluency.

When introducing a play to students, read aloud the whole play first, making sure to pay close attention to phrasing, pacing, and expression. Students need to hear a model of fluent reading to develop their own fluency skills.

2. Let students practice reading independently.

Encourage students to read the script independently so they can focus on the text and identify new vocabulary words and practice decoding unfamiliar words. Help individual students as needed.

3. Give students practice reading in groups.

Invite students to practice reading aloud in their groups. When students listen to one another read and get feedback from both their peers and you, their accuracy and fluency improves. As they begin to read automatically, they can start thinking about how to interpret their parts for the audience. Encourage students to think about how to use their voice and actions to make their characters come to life.

4. Have students perform to an audience.

This is the moment everybody's been waiting for! Invite each group to stand in front of the class and read aloud its play. Then sit back and enjoy your students' performance.

After all the groups have performed, consider throwing a "cast party" to celebrate your confident and fluent readers!

Can the Thrilling Three Save Grandville?

Characters

Narrator 1
Narrator 2
Flexor
X-Spec
Rocket
The Bungler
Questioner
Match-Head

Narrator 1: The Thrilling Three were a team of superheroes. The Rocket could fly at tremendous speeds. Flexor was very stretchy. X-Spec had special vision for seeing through walls. Their job was to protect Grandville from evil.

Narrator 2: A bad man named the Bungler was trying to get away. He raced through the city, and the Thrilling Three chased after him.

Flexor: The Bungler is going really fast.

X-Spec: It looks like he is riding on his superfast, jet-powered unicycle.

Rocket: I wonder where he is going. I'm sure he is up to no good.

The Bungler: Ha-ha! There's only one of me. I have only one wheel on my unicycle. But I bet you still can't catch me, Thrilling Three.

Rocket: Flexor and X-Spec, hold on to my wings. I am going to fly really fast.

Flexor: Oh no. I cannot see him anymore. We seem to have lost him.

X-Spec: I'll just turn on my X-ray vision. Let me scan around. I'm looking through that building, and I have spotted him on the other side.

Narrator 1: Flexor's rubber arm shot out and snaked around to the other side of the building. Flexor's hand grabbed a telephone pole and yanked the Thrilling Three around the corner. Now they were right behind the Bungler once again.

Flexor: This is a busy street. There are people walking everywhere. We have to be careful.

Rocket: I am going to fly up higher in the sky. We cannot catch the Bungler here. A person might get hurt.

X-Spec: I'll keep my eyes focused on the Bungler. He can't escape my gaze. We'll follow him from up in the sky.

Narrator 2: The Thrilling Three followed the Bungler down the busy street. Suddenly, the Bungler stopped. A garage door opened and he rode inside.

Rocket: We have to hurry. Hold on tight. I am coming in for a landing.

X-Spec: Make haste. I can see directly through the roof of the building. The Bungler is trying to shut the garage door.

Flexor: I will just send one of my long arms inside the garage. There. I just pressed the button to make the door go back up.

Narrator 1: The Thrilling Three ran into the garage. The Bungler was ready for them. He was standing behind a weird machine that looked kind of like a telescope. He pushed a button and out shot a ray of light.

Narrator 2: The Bungler shot each of the Thrilling Three with the ray. Now each one was trapped in a block of ice.

Bungler: Ha-ha, Thrilling Three. Or should I say, Chilling Three. I knew you would follow me. Now you have fallen right into my trap.

I'm going to the top of Tall Tower. I have a special whistle set up there. It is incredibly unpleasant sounding. It doesn't bother me. I'm not human. When humans hear it, they all have to cover their ears.

I'll be able to rob banks. I'll be able to steal cars. No one can stop me. This is going to be so much fun. Hey, superheroes! Stay cool! Ha-ha-ha-ha!

Questioner: What will happen next? Will the Bungler get away with his evil plan? Will he turn on that horrible whistle, make people cover their ears in pain, then steal everything in Grandville? Will dogs actually like the whistle and start dancing?

Or will the Thrilling Three escape from their icy cells? (If you guessed that, you're getting warmer!) Will they be able to save Grandville from the Bungler? How many questions will I ask? What do you think will happen next?

Narrator 1: You probably didn't expect this to happen! (Well, maybe you did expect it, if you read the whole list of characters at the beginning.) Match-Head walked into the garage. He was a very unpopular superhero. He was a skinny man with a tiny head that could burst into flame just like a match. All he was really good for was starting fires and lighting fuses. The Thrilling Three always tried to avoid Match-Head.

Match-Head: Oh boy! Oh my! What has happened? What is happening? What do I do? What do I do?

Narrator 2: Then Match-Head had an idea. He stood beside X-Spec. Match-Head's tiny head burst into flame. The block of ice began to melt.

X-Spec: Way to use your noggin, Match-Head. Now go stand beside Flexor and Rocket and defrost them, too.

Flexor: Thanks for getting me out of that ice, Match-Head.

Rocket: Thanks. Now we have to hurry to Tall Tower. Hold onto my wings everybody. That includes you, Match-Head.

Narrator 1: The four superheroes blasted through the air and landed on Tall Tower. They jumped into the building through a window. Then they started running up and down the halls searching for the Bungler.

Rocket: Where is he? We have to find him before he starts that horrible whistle.

X-Spec: I'm looking through the walls. There he is! He's inside of that room directly down the hall.

Flexor: The door is locked. I will make my arm as thin as paper. Now I will slide it under the door. There. I got it. I have unlocked the door.

Match-Head: It is dark in here. The Bungler must have turned out the lights. I'll just fire up my head. Good. Now we can see.

Rocket: There he is! Grab him!

Narrator 2: The four seized the Bungler. They were able to stop him right before he set off the whistle. Grandville was saved. The Bungler went to jail.

Match-Head: I really helped you all. Can I join your team now?

Flexor: Sorry, Match-Head. We would like you to join. But you cannot.

X-Spec: You see, our name is the Thrilling Three. If you joined, there would be four of us. People would make fun of a team called the Thrilling Three with four people in it.

Narrator 1: That made sense to Match-Head. If he could find a team that needed a fourth member, it would be fantastic!

Will Erin Win the Third Annual Willow Grove French Fry Eating Contest?

Characters

Narrator 1
Narrator 2
Announcer
Erin
James
Alice-Nicole
Crowd (at least two people)
Questioner

Narrator 1: The town of Willow Grove was holding its third annual french fry eating contest. This year there were three kids competing. The winner would get the mystery prize.

Narrator 2: Erin was way smaller than the other two kids. She could not eat nearly as much. She could not eat nearly as fast. But she knew she needed to find a way. Erin wanted to win.

Announcer: Welcome everyone to this year's french fry eating contest. Let's go over the rules. You have five minutes to eat as many french fries as you can.

Each of you will start out with a plate of french fries. It has exactly 50 fries on it. If you finish one plate of fries, we will bring you another plate. The winner is the one who eats the most french fries. That person will win a fantastic mystery prize.

Remember, no throwing up. That's an automatic disqualification. If french fries come out of your nose, you will also be disqualified. Finally, you may not hide a hungry puppy under the table and secretly feed him your fries.

Erin: This is a humongous helping of fries. I don't even know how I can finish one plate. But I'll have to find a way. I want that prize!

James: For me, one plate of fries is a tiny snack. I usually eat about five times this many fries with a meal. I also have four cheeseburgers, some chicken planks, a bowl of chili, an apple pie, and a giant-size milk shake. That's just my breakfast. I'm going to win this contest.

Alice-Nicole: This is too easy. I can eat a whole plate in about one minute. I don't just mean the food. I mean the plate. I'm hungry today. I may have to eat the table.

Announcer: Are you ready, contestants? On your mark, get set, go!

Crowd: Eat those fries! Eat those fries! Chew, chew, chew! Yum, yum, yum!

Narrator 1: Alice-Nicole jumped out to an early lead. She finished her first plate of fries at record speed. Erin wondered if she really would eat the plate. James was right behind Alice-Nicole, wolfing down fries.

Narrator 2: Erin was in last place. She was eating very slowly. She had to think of some way to catch up with the others. Erin decided to make a funny face.

Erin: Hey, look at me. I'm crossing my eyes, sticking out my tongue, and making a pig nose all at the same time. Check out the tip of my tongue. There's a little piece of half-chewed french fry.

James: (*mouth full*) Nice try, Erin. There's no way you can distract me. I'm in the eating zone right now. I remember one time I was at a picnic and a huge thunderstorm started.

Everyone ran for shelter. But I sat out in the rain and ate six peanut butter and jelly sandwiches and four chocolate chip cookies. That food was soaking wet. But it was still delicious.

Alice-Nicole: (*mouth full*) I am doing so well that I think I will stop and look at your funny face. That is pretty good, Erin. Now someone bring me two new plates at the same time! I am starving!

Announcer: Alice-Nicole has a commanding lead at this point. James is in second, but coming on strong. Erin is a distant third.
Two minutes have elapsed, contestants. Three minutes remain.

Crowd: Eat more fries! Eat more fries! Stuff your mouths! Gobble them up!

Narrator 1: Erin was falling further and further behind. The contest was nearly halfway over. Even if Alice-Nicole and James stopped eating right then, they had such massive leads that Erin would never catch them. But she wanted that prize.

Narrator 2: Erin knew she needed to come up with another plan. She decided to say some really gross things about the food. Maybe that would make the other two kids sick. They might not be able to eat anymore. Then Erin could win.

Erin: Have you ever noticed that french fries look kind of like big yellow caterpillars? I bet they taste pretty similar, too. I'm guessing that a caterpillar is crunchy on the outside and all mushy inside. Just think about it! It's really pretty gross!

James: (*mouth full*) Nice try, Erin. I have a really strong stomach. Nothing really grosses me out. I remember one time I dipped a potato chip into a bowl full of something that I thought was sour cream dip.

It turned out to be cottage cheese. But I didn't mind. Potato chips and cottage cheese are a good combination. Chips also taste good with either honey or applesauce.

Alice-Nicole: (*mouth full*) I am so far in the lead that I think I will stop and think about what you just said. Let's see, Erin. Do fries taste like bugs? Maybe bugs taste great! I am really not sure. I really do not care. What I do know is that I am hungry! Someone bring me three more plates!

Announcer: This is incredible, folks! There is exactly one minute left. Alice-Nicole has a chance to eat a thousand fries. She may set a new record. James is still a strong second and Erin remains a distant third.

Crowd: Eat, eat, eat! Munch, munch, munch! Crunch, crunch, crunch!

Questioner: What will happen next? Will Erin think of a new plan? Will it work? Is there any way that Erin can catch up? Will she use ketchup? And what if she actually won? Would she be the chomp champ? What is the mystery prize anyway? Do I ask too many questions?

Narrator 1: The clock was ticking. There was less than a minute left and Erin was desperately behind.

Narrator 2: But then an idea came to Erin. Tell a joke! That might just work. It sure was worth a try.

Erin: Listen to this. What did the snail say when he was riding on the turtle's back? Think about it. Are you ready for the answer? The snail said, "Slow down or you'll get a ticket."

James: (*mouth full*) Ha-ha-ha-ha.

Alice-Nicole: (*mouth full*) Ha-ha-ha-ha.

Announcer: Ha-ha-ha-ha.

Crowd: Ha-ha-ha-ha.

Narrator 1: Once James and Alice-Nicole started laughing, they couldn't stop. Soon they were laughing hysterically. Tears streamed down their faces. And then it happened. French fries came out of their noses. They were both instantly disqualified.

Narrator 2: Erin could not believe it! Her plan had worked! She was the winner. She could not wait to find out what prize she had won.

Announcer: Congratulations, young lady. You have won the third annual Willow Grove French Fry Eating Contest.

Thanks to some clever and unconventional tactics, you figured out a way to come from behind and win. It was a thrilling victory.

And now it is time to reveal the mystery prize. I think you will be very pleased. You have won a lifetime supply of . . . french fries!

Will Isabella's Time Machine Work?

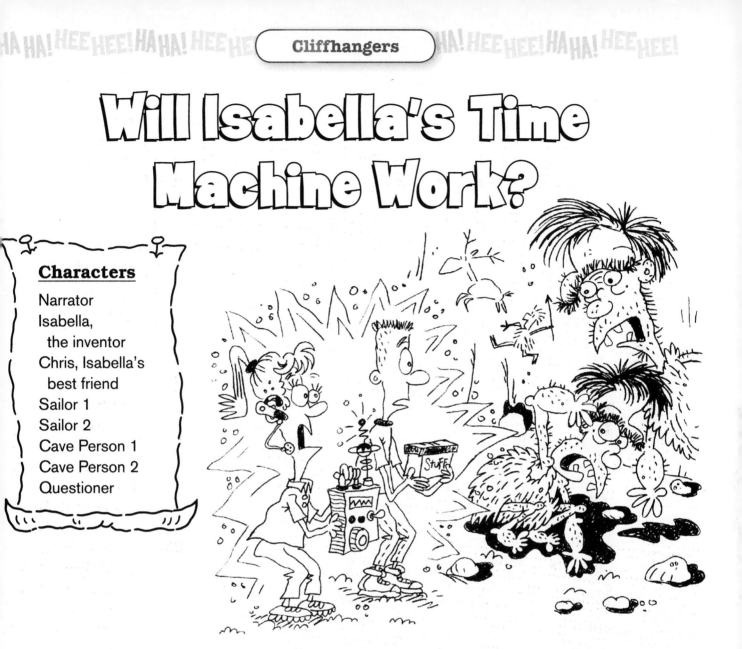

Characters

Narrator
Isabella,
  the inventor
Chris, Isabella's
  best friend
Sailor 1
Sailor 2
Cave Person 1
Cave Person 2
Questioner

Narrator: Isabella was the most talented inventor in the fifth grade. She had won blue ribbons at the school science fair three years in a row.

Isabella had an exciting new invention. It was a machine that was supposed to make it possible to travel in time. She could go back to the year 1900, or even back to the time of princes and princesses.

The machine was small, about the size of a portable music player. When she traveled through time, Isabella planned to carry the machine with her. She decided to test it out with her best friend, Chris. He was bringing a little box of common items from the modern world. It would be fun to show the items to people they met when they traveled into the past.

Isabella: If I just turn this knob and push this button, we should travel through time.

Chris: What part of the past are we going to visit? Are we going back to when there were dinosaurs on earth?

Isabella: No, I don't want to go back that far yet. This is the first time we've ever tried this time machine. So I'm aiming for around the 1700s. Are you ready?

Chris: I am as ready as I will ever be. Let's do some time-traveling!

Narrator: Isabella turned the knob and clicked the button on the time machine. There was a bright flash of light. An instant later the two friends found themselves on a ship in the middle of the sea.

Sailor 1: Hey, look. There are two kids on our ship. Where do you think they came from?

Sailor 2: Ahoy, there! Identify yourselves you slinking, scurvy dogs.

Isabella: We are stowaways. We have been hiding down below, but we just decided to come up on deck.

Chris: (*whispering*) What a great fib, Isabella. That is the way to think fast on your feet.

Narrator: Isabella and Chris could not help noticing that one sailor had a peg leg. The other wore an eye patch.
    When the sailors spoke, the two friends caught a whiff of their foul breath. These were some filthy, stinky sailors.

Sailor 1: These two have been hiding on our ship the whole time we have been at sea. What should we do?

Sailor 2: Aye, you two wanted a taste of the seafaring life. What do you say we put you to work? Do you think you can make yourselves useful aboard a ship?

Isabella: Sure. I'm ready for an exciting adventure.

Chris: Count me in. What do you want us to do?

Sailor 1: For your first job, you can help us raise the ship's flag.

Sailor 2: Grab ahold of those ropes you pair of miserable landlubbers. Help us hoist the Jolly Roger.

Narrator: Isabella and Chris raised the flag. But the moment it began to flap in the ocean breeze, they were filled with terror. The flag was black, with a skull and crossbones. The time machine had landed them smack on the deck of a pirate ship!

Chris: (*whispering*) I am scared. What are we going to do? We have to get out of here.

Isabella: (*whispering*) Why don't you create a distraction. Maybe you can give the pirates something from the box you brought along. While you're doing that, I'll pull the time machine out of my pocket. I think I may be able to get us back to where we came from.

Chris: Hey, mateys! That is a great flag. Would you like to try my friend's new invention? They're called breath mints. Here, try one. That's right. Just chew them up.

Sailor 1: This sure tastes good.

Sailor 2: Arrgghhh! Minty fresh!

Narrator: Just as the pirates finished their breath mints, there was a flash of white light. Isabella and Chris disappeared from the ship.

An instant later, the two friends reappeared. They were inside a cave. Paintings of deer and other wild animals covered the cave's walls. Two people were crouched in the corner.

Chris: How did we end up here? I thought we were going to go back to the present time. And who are those hairy people?

Isabella: I think they're cave people. I must have entered the wrong settings on the time machine. Instead of winding up in the modern world, we have traveled even further back in time.

Fortunately, I am prepared. I brought my portable Neanderthal-translation microphone. Do you remember this, Chris? It won a blue ribbon in last year's science fair. Here, I'll just turn this on and we should be able to understand what they are saying.

Cave person 1: Who are you? Why do you look so strange?

Cave person 2: What are you? Why aren't you covered in hair? Why do you have such teeny foreheads? Are you actually people or are you some other kind of creatures?

Chris: I know we look different from you. Please don't be scared. We are also people. We live in caves far away from here. We are lost.

Isabella: (*whispering*) Way to think quickly on your feet, Chris. I think they are convinced by your story.

Cave person 1: I am sorry that you are lost. You must be very tired and very hungry.

Cave person 2: Hey look! The hunters have returned. Let's help them drag that huge beast into the cave. I hope you two will join us for a feast. We will dine well tonight.

Questioner: What do you think happened next? What kind of animal was it? Did Chris and Isabella help eat it? Or did they simply use their machine to get away? Were they able to return to the present? Or did they stay lost in time? Do cave people need breath mints too?

Isabella: I believe the huge animal that they are dragging is a woolly mammoth. Now, I know we've never tried mammoth. But something makes me think we would not enjoy it.

Chris, why don't you get something out of your box. Maybe you can create a distraction. I'll program the time machine so that we can be out of here before dinner.

Narrator: Chris fished around in the box and found a quarter. Then Chris left the cave, bringing along the portable Neanderthal-translation microphone. A large group of cave people continued to drag the huge woolly mammoth.

Chris: I see that you are all dragging this animal. It seems very heavy. Look what I have in my hand. It is a small circle.

Let's find some rocks that are this kind of shape. Then we can build something that rolls like this small circle. We can place the animal on the wagon. Then it will be much easier to move.

Narrator: Chris helped the cave people to start building a wagon to move the mammoth. Meanwhile, Isabella fiddled with the time machine. She figured out the mistake she had made earlier. She had turned a knob backward intending to go back to the present time. To return to the present, she realized they needed to go forward in time.

Now Isabella had the time machine programmed properly. There was a flash of light and she and Chris disappeared. They returned safely to modern times. Isabella ended up winning a blue ribbon for her time machine. Meanwhile, the cave people appreciated the help.

Cave person 1: I wonder what ever happened to those two people. They seem to have just disappeared.

Cave person 2: I'm glad they stuck around long enough to teach us that great trick. It sure makes life easier. Hey, I just thought of a great name. Let's call it a greel.

Cave person 1: "Greel" is a silly name. How about a smeel?

Cave person 2: I don't like the sound of "smeel." How about a preel?

Cave person 1: We'll think of a name later.

Cave person 2: I agree. I'm sure there's a name that will really roll off of the tongue.

There's Always an Explanation

Characters

Narrator 1
Narrator 2
Mr. Blackmore
Mrs. Blackmore
Liz
Thornton
  Blackmore
Spooky voice
Suit of Armor

Narrator 1: Liz was visiting her cousin, Thornton. He lived in a big old house. The house was dark and creepy. At night, there were always lots of strange noises.

Narrator 2: Liz's parents had sent her to stay for the weekend. But she never liked visiting the Blackmores. It seemed like they made a special effort to act spooky. Who else had a suit of knight's armor standing in the hallway? What other 11-year-old boy was named Thornton?

Mr. Blackmore: Welcome to our home, Liz. You have arrived just in time. I think a big thunderstorm is about to begin. We are so glad you will be staying for the weekend.

Mrs. Blackmore: Thornton, can you help Liz carry her suitcase upstairs? I thought we would have you stay in the big room on the third floor. It is the room with the long flowing curtains. You love sleeping there, right?

Liz: Uh, yeah. It's a really . . . cheery room.

Thornton: C'mon, Liz. We'll carry your suitcase up to your room. Then I will show you my new pet toad. Other kids like dogs and cats and gerbils. I prefer toads. They make such delightful companions.

Narrator 1: Liz stopped by her big, dark, spooky room. She went with Thornton to look at his new pet toad. Then it was time for dinner.

Narrator 2: As with everything else at the Blackmore house, dinner was strange. What other family ate every meal at a long table with tall candles? Who were all those somber-looking people in paintings on the wall?

Mr. Blackmore: Could you please pass me a bowl of soup?

Mrs. Blackmore: Hold on a moment, dear. Let me just finish cutting up the main course.

Liz: What kind of soup are we having? And what is the main course?

Mr. Blackmore: The main coarse is wild boar. Don't you just love the rotten apple in its mouth? As for the soup, it's mushroom. We found the mushrooms in the basement behind the washing machine. How does that sound?

Liz: That sounds . . . really good. I just wish I had more of an appetite. But I already ate dinner on the airplane ride here. I think I'll just have another piece of bread.

Thornton: It's your loss, Liz. It just means more mushroom soup and wild boar for me. That looks scrumptious, Mom. I know I'll want seconds.

Narrator 1: After dinner, Mr. Blackmore read a story to Liz and Thornton. He called it a bedtime story. But it was a pretty scary story. It was about a ghost that lived in an old house. Then Liz went up to her room. The storm had started. Liz did not feel tired now. She was wide awake.

Narrator 2: Big flashes of lightning lit up her room. Thunder rattled the windows. It seemed to Liz like everything about the Blackmore house was spooky.

The really annoying part was that they seemed to enjoy making their visitors uncomfortable. Liz pulled the covers up to her chin. Suddenly, she heard this eerie voice.

Spooky voice: Beware. Be afraid. You are not safe. You cannot see me. You cannot stop me. I will have revenge. You can hide. But I will find you. I will get you.

Narrator 1: Who was that talking in a scary voice? What was that voice? It was not anyone in the Blackmore family. Liz was very scared. She jumped out of her bed and ran into the hall.

Liz: Help! Wake up everybody! Some kind of goblin is loose in the house.

Mr. Blackmore: I'm so sorry, Liz. I was simply watching a horror movie. It just seemed like the perfect night. With all the thunder, I guess I turned up the volume too loud. But I certainly didn't mean to scare you.

Mrs. Blackmore: He loves to watch his silly old movies. I guess this one gave you a bit of scare. Ha-ha-ha-ha.

Thornton: Did you really believe there was a goblin in our house? You know, Liz, there's always an explanation for anything that happens.

Narrator 1: Liz went back to her room. The storm grew stronger. The shadows grew longer. Several hours of night passed in the Blackmore house. She tried to sleep. But she could not.

Narrator 2: Suddenly, she heard this weird clanking sound in the hall. She gathered all her courage. She got out of bed and tiptoed to the door. She peeked out into the hallway. A suit of armor was walking around!

Suit of armor: I will do battle. I will fight in the name of my king. I will risk my life for my queen. I will save this land!

Liz: Wake up everybody! The armor has come to life.

Mr. Blackmore: I'm so sorry, Liz. I should have warned you. That is our butler, Mr. Bartholomew. He is playing a knight in an upcoming theatrical production. We told him he could wear the armor when he rehearses his lines. We certainly didn't mean to scare you.

Liz: But it's the middle of the night! A humongous thunderstorm is going on and he's practicing lines for his play.

Mrs. Blackmore: He works during the day, Liz. This is the only time he has to himself. What a night! Or I should say, what a knight! Ha-ha-ha-ha.

Liz: I didn't even know you had a butler!

Thornton: We just hired him. He was doing some work down in the basement when you arrived. He found the mushrooms. So now you know. You realize, Liz, that's there's always an explanation for anything that happens.

Narrator 1: Liz did not sleep at all that night. The next night there was another storm. Mr. Blackmore told another scary story. But Liz planned to make sure she got a good night's rest. She planned to do everything she could to ignore the strange ways of the Blackmore family.

Narrator 2: Liz put a special white beauty cream on her face. It was a gift from her grandma. She figured it would make her feel better in this very spooky house. Then she put in some earplugs. A stewardess had handed them out during her airplane ride.

    There. She was feeling better already. The only problem was she was really hungry after avoiding all the bizarre food served by the Blackmores. It sounded like everyone else was asleep. So she decided to sneak down to the kitchen for a snack. Thornton heard her walking down the steps. He came out of his room to see who it was.

Thornton: Liz? Liz? Is that you? Liz? Liz? Hey, why won't you answer me? If it's really you, Liz, answer me!

Narrator 1: Liz kept walking down the stairs. As she went, Thornton got a look at her face. It was bright white!

Thornton: Mom, Dad, help! Cousin Liz isn't human. She's some kind of terrifying ghost creature.

Mr. Blackmore: Oh no! There's a poltergeist in our midst! Run, hide!

Mrs. Blackmore: This is not funny. No, this is not funny at all. I'm getting very scared, dear.

Narrator 2: Out of the corner of her eye, Liz suddenly realized there was a big commotion. She took out her earplugs. She turned her very white face toward the frightened Blackmores.

Mr. Blackmore: Liz, is that really you?

Liz: I'm sorry, everybody. I couldn't hear you at first. The storm was keeping me awake. So I put in these earplugs to shut out the sound. I was going downstairs to get a snack. I guess I left them in.

Thornton: But your face! What's happened to your face? It's so frightfully pale and ghostly!

Liz: Nothing, silly. I'm just wearing some beauty cream my grandma gave me for my birthday. I sure didn't mean to scare you. You know, Thornton, there's always an explanation for everything.

A Ghost at the Gifford School

Characters

Narrator 1
Narrator 2
Cody
Juan
Laura
Aaron
Michelle
Mrs. Fletcher

Narrator 1: Cody had never behaved strangely before. He liked pizza and soccer, the same as the other kids at the Gifford School.

Then one day, he started claiming that he was friends with a ghost. None of the other kids saw any evidence that this ghost even existed.

Narrator 2: Every place that Cody went, he said the ghost was there, too. He even saved a seat at lunch for this ghost. He always put out a plate of food.

Cody: Hey, watch what you are doing. You almost sat right on top of Maximillian.

Juan: Oh, I'm so sorry Maximillian. I didn't see you there.

You know why I didn't see him, Cody? Because he's not there! Ghosts aren't real. He doesn't exist. So why are you saving a seat at the lunch table? This is getting ridiculous! And what kind of name is Maximillian anyway? If I made up a ghost, at least I'd come up with a cool name.

Cody: Stop it, Juan. You're hurting Maximillian's feelings.

Laura: It does not look like your friend is eating, Cody. He has not touched his turkey sandwich. He has not had a bite of his corn.

Cody: I guess he is not very hungry today. I don't think he likes turkey.

Juan: Hey, let me have his brownie!

Laura: Here comes Sheila. She needs a place to sit. Cody, can you at least ask Maximillian to move.

Narrator 1: Saving a seat at lunch for a ghost was bad enough. But then Cody insisted that the ghost should play on his soccer team at recess. Now the kids were really starting to lose their patience.

Aaron: This is not fair. Our team has four players. The other team has five. How are we going to score any points?

Cody: That is not true, Aaron. We have five players, too. For some reason none of the rest of you can see Maximillian. Trust me. He is here. You should all be happy. Maximillian is great at this game.

Michelle: If he's so great, maybe he should play goalie instead of me. We can just let the other team score whenever they please. I just love the idea of losing by about a gazillion points.

Aaron: Let's just play the game. Are you ready, Cody? I am going to kick the ball to you.

Cody: Got it. Now get open, Max! Great move. Here comes the ball. I'm kicking it your way.

Narrator 2: The ball just kept rolling. When Cody kicked the ball, there was no one there to stop it. The ball rolled right off the field. It finally came to a rest beside some first graders who were jumping rope.

Cody: Sorry about that. I will go pick up the ball.

Michelle: Why doesn't Maximillian go get it? He's the big soccer superstar.
I don't see how he could have missed that, Cody. You kicked it right to him. That was him, right? It looked like thin air to me. But I don't have special powers to see ghosts. Ooooh, so spooky!

Cody: Max tripped when I kicked the ball to him, Michelle. That is why he did not get it. He is brushing himself off right now. If you will excuse me, I am going to go get the ball.

Aaron: Let's calm down everybody. We have a game to play. And right now we do not have a ghost of a chance. Sorry, I just could not help saying that.

Narrator 1: Cody was clinging to his ghost story. But nobody else had seen one ounce of proof.
In the classroom, Cody asked if Maximillian could have a place to sit. The teacher, Mrs. Fletcher, said he could use Kim's desk. Kim was sick and had stayed home from school that day. Everyone in the class snickered. This was getting truly loopy.

Juan: Mrs. Fletcher, is it okay if I bring my werewolf buddy to school tomorrow?

Aaron: I do not know what is wrong with Cody. We lost our game, 28–0. There is no one sitting in that seat.

Michelle: I think Maximillian is chewing gum, Mrs. Fletcher. I can't see him, of course. But I believe I hear him chomping. You always say that students who chew gum had better have enough to share with the whole class.

Laura: Can I go sit at Kim's desk today? I can see better from there.

Mrs. Fletcher: Please stay where you are, Laura. Calm down, everyone.

Let's concentrate on our lessons. Now, can anyone tell me the name of a mammal that also lays eggs? Remember, almost all mammals give birth to live young. But there are two rare mammals that lay eggs. Anyone?

Cody: Maximillian has his hand raised, Mrs. Fletcher. Please could you call on him?

Mrs. Fletcher: I am going to humor you just this one time, Cody. Maximillian, can you name one of the two mammals that lay eggs?

Narrator 2: For a few seconds nothing happened. Then, a piece of chalk floated up into the air. All the children gasped. The chalk began to write words.

Mrs. Fletcher: Duck-billed platypus. That is the correct answer. Oh my. I feel faint. I think I am going to have to sit down for a spell.

Cody: None of you believed me. See I told you. Max is my friend. And he is real!

Narrator 1: When Kim came back to class, Maximillian was given his own desk. He actually started eating lunch. It was strange to watch the food simply disappear.

Having a ghost in school certainly took some getting used to. But the kids grew to like Maximillian, even if only Cody could see him. He was a lot of fun to have around.

Narrator 2: About the only thing the kids did not enjoy was playing soccer with Maximillian. He was a real ghost. That was true. But there was another thing that was true. Maximillian was very bad at soccer.

A People Story

Characters

Narrator 1
Narrator 2
Grog,
  camp counselor
Blap, assistant
  camp counselor
Ick,
  young monster
Trigor,
  young monster
Snink,
  young monster
Driffle,
  young monster

Narrator 1: Do you ever wonder what scares monsters? Do you wonder what kind of scary stories they tell? They tell people stories, of course!

Narrator 2: Some young monsters went camping in the woods. They played all night. But then the sun began to rise. Daylight is a scary time for monsters.

  The young monsters were a little nervous. They gathered around a big pile of rotting moss. That's what monsters have instead of campfires. Then the older monsters told a people story.

Grog: Are you ready monster campers? I'm going to tell you a terrifying people story. It was early one morning. A young person was just waking up. He slept on a long clean platform called a bed.

He lived inside a big box called a house. The scariest part: This house had windows, and it was full of bright light!

Ick: What was he called? What was the person's name?

Blap: The person's name was . . . Jeff!

Trigor: That's a bizarre name. What did this Jeff look like? Did he have hands with long skinny fingers? Did he have clean nails rather than filthy claws? Did he have teeth instead of fangs?

Grog: Yes, Jeff had ten fingers with clean, recently washed nails. When he opened his mouth, it was full of teeth that weren't very sharp. His ears were round, not pointed. He did not have horns, wings, or warts. But here is the truly scary part: Jeff had exactly two eyes. And they were blue!

Snink: He had two blue eyes! That's the weirdest thing I've ever heard. He didn't have three eyes like me? His eyes weren't yellow like Ick's or bloodshot like Trigor's.

Driffle: I'm scared. I want to go home.

Blap: Don't worry. It is just a story.

Grog: Jeff got onto a vehicle called a bike. A bike has two wheels, and it rolls. He went to a place called a school. Schools are full of young people.

Ick: Are there ten people in a school? Or are there even more? Are there twenty people in a school?

Blap: Sometimes there are as many as a thousand people in a school.

Trigor: That's the scariest thing I've ever heard. I can't even imagine a thousand people in one place. What if a monster got trapped in a school?

Snink: Just think about all those people. They would all be walking, and they would have two eyes and teeth that weren't sharp. I bet they would not have fur, either.

Blap: That is right. People don't have fur. They have small amounts of hair on top of their heads.

Driffle: Now I am so scared. Please just tell a nice happy ghost story.

Blap: Don't worry, Driffle. This is just pretend. People are not real.

Grog: Let's continue our story. When the sun was very bright Jeff was ready to eat. He went to a place called the school cafeteria. It was full of hungry people!

Remember, people have hands not claws. But they don't even eat with their hands. They use strange tools called forks, knives, and spoons.

Ick: What did Jeff eat?

Grog: Jeff ate something called spaghetti. It's a long skinny type of food and it is covered in a red sauce.

Ick: Is the red sauce blood? I like blood!

Blap: No, the red sauce that Jeff ate was made from tomatoes.

Trigor: Jeff killed a tomato! People are so scary. They attack sweet innocent vegetables in the middle of the day and gobble them up.

Grog: Yes, Jeff was also eating corn with his spaghetti. He was drinking a brown liquid called chocolate milk.

Ick: Is chocolate milk like mud? I love mud.

Blap: It looks like mud. But it tastes kind of sweet.

Snink: Yuck. I hate sweet flavors. Boy, I would be so scared if I ran into a two-eyed, ten-fingered, chocolate milk–drinking person on a sunny day. I don't know what I'd do.

Grog: But just hold on. Are you ready? Here's the truly scary part. Jeff and the other young people remained in the school all through the bright, sunny afternoon. Then it was time to go home. A device called a bell made a blood-curdling sound.

Ick: What did it sound like? What sound does a bell make?

Narrator 1: Now Blap was ready to play a trick. He had snuck off into the woods.

Narrator 2: Earlier in the night, Blap had discovered a rusty tin can in the woods. This was something Blap had never seen before. When the monster had tried hitting the can with a stick, it had made a frightening sound. Now Blap was waiting for Grog to give him the signal.

Grog: What does a bell sound like, little monsters? It sounds just like this . . .

Narrator 1: Blap hit the old can with the stick. It made a ringing sound.

Ick: Aaaaaaah! Help, help! There's a person in the woods.

Trigor: That sound! It's hideous. It's making my pointed ears ache and twitch.

Snink: I think I can smell the person. The smell is wafting from that direction. The odor is getting closer.

Driffle: Wah-wah! I just want to go home. I want my monster mommy!

Narrator 2: Just then, Blap came out of the woods. He had given the campers a good scare. It took a while for everyone to calm down. They all had a warm glass of mud and some moldy bread. Then the monster campers climbed into their holes in the ground. It was time for bed. The morning sun was getting high in the sky.

The Case of the Disappearing Hats

Characters

Narrator 1
Steph, a student
Dante, the school
  detective
Narrator 2
Shopkeeper 1
Shopkeeper 2
Shopkeeper 3
Nathan, the hat
  thief

Narrator 1: Kids at Grovetown Elementary kept losing their hats. It always happened when they were walking home from school, and it always happened under the same bridge.

One moment, the hat would be sitting snugly on a kid's head. The next moment, it would fly straight up into the air and disappear. Already, three different kids had lost their hats this way. When it happened yet again, it was time for Dante, Grovetown Elementary's student detective.

Steph: The hat thief has hit again. It happened to me last night. Someone took my ball cap right off my head.

Dante: I'm sorry to hear that, Steph. Now take your time. Try to remember exactly what happened. Don't leave out any details. They could be crucial.

Steph: I was walking home from school. I walked under the bridge. I was wearing my hat. Then it felt like someone was pulling it off my head.

Here is the strange thing. I was all by myself. There was no one else around. My hat went straight up into the air. Then it disappeared.

Narrator 2: This sure was odd, thought Dante. It sounded like some kind of trick. He had cracked many cases before. So Dante had some tricks of his own.

He decided to visit some stores in Grovetown. He planned to ask some questions. That might give him some clues. The first store Dante visited was a food market.

Dante: Good evening. I just wanted to ask you a few questions. It will only take a moment.

Have you noticed anything strange lately? Have any kids visited your grocery store and bought any unusual items?

Shopkeeper 1: Kids come in here all the time. They buy fruit and candy and soda. But no one has stood out. No kid has bought anything that was strange.

Dante: Thank you for the information. Here is my card with my cell phone number. Please call me if you see anything suspicious.

Shopkeeper 1: Wait kid. If you come into a store, you should buy something.

Dante: OK, fine. I will buy one mango, please.

Narrator 1: Dante continued his investigation. He continued to walk down the main street of Grovetown.

Dante: Hello. If you have a minute, I have a few quick questions for you. I'm investigating a series of mysterious hat disappearances.

Have you seen anything unusual lately? Have any kids visited your toy store and made any odd purchases?

Shopkeeper 2: Let me think about that for a moment. Let's see. I've had lots of kids buy Zoom City toy cars lately. Those are always very popular with little boys. I've been selling a ton of Burp-a-Bye Baby dolls. Those are a huge hit with little girls.

Dante: Think hard. Did any one kid stand out? Of all the children who visit your toy store, is there one that grabbed your attention in particular?

Shopkeeper 2: Why, yes. Now that you mention it, a boy came in a couple of weeks ago and bought some kite string. That seemed a little strange.

Dante: Why is that?

Shopkeeper 2: For one thing, it's springtime now. I never sell kites during this time of year. Everyone buys them in the fall, when it is windy.

For another thing, the boy only bought kite string. He didn't buy a kite. It kind of made me wonder.

Dante: What did this boy look like?

Shopkeeper 2: He was skinny with black hair.

Dante: Thank you for the lead. Here is my card and cell phone number. Call me if you think of any other important details.

Shopkeeper 2: Listen, kid. I don't mind answering all your questions. But the least you can do is buy something from my store. That would be polite.

Dante: I suppose so. Let's see, I will buy a tube of model glue.

Narrator 2: This was good information. It was worth buying the glue. Dante left the toy store. He walked down the street. His next stop was the pet store.

Dante: Greetings. I'm conducting a missing-hat investigation. I need to ask you a few questions. It will only take a few minutes out of your busy evening.

Have you seen anything weird lately? Have any kids come into your store recently and made surprising pet choices?

Shopkeeper 3: Hmmm. We have sold kids a lot of puppies lately. We've sold lots of kittens. Tropical fish are a big seller this spring. But these are very common pets, right?

Dante: That's right. But maybe there's one kid who bought something unusual, like a shark or a falcon. Think about it.

Shopkeeper 3: Hold on a minute. I'm remembering something. A kid came in here a couple of weeks ago and bought a lizard. It was a gecko.

That's not our most popular pet. We sell a few here and there. But there was just something odd about this boy.

Dante: What was that?

Shopkeeper 3: He just kept asking all these questions about how sticky the gecko's toes were. Can a gecko stick to glass? Can a gecko stick to plastic? Can a gecko stick to cloth? All that seemed to concern him was how sticky the gecko's feet were.

Dante: Do you happen to recall anything about this boy's appearance?

Shopkeeper 3: Yes. He was really skinny and he had really dark black hair.

Dante: You've been a great help. Thank you. Here is my card with my cell phone number. Call me if you think of anything else.

Shopkeeper 3: You know, kid, it's important to be polite when you are in a store.

Dante: You don't have to explain. I will buy the hat that says "I love my pet ferret."

Narrator 2: Dante had gathered some excellent information. Now he had a pretty good idea of who was stealing hats. He also had a pretty good idea of how the person was doing it.

After school, Dante sat in the playground. He has wearing his new hat. Dante made some special changes to the hat.

Dante was waiting for the suspect. He planned to confront him. He planned to ask some questions that would cause the suspect to reveal his guilt.

Dante: Hi, Nathan. This is frustrating! My shoes won't stay tied! No matter what I do, the laces always come loose. I trip over them.

Nathan: It is easy to tie good knots. I will show you.

Narrator 1: Nathan leaned down and tied Dante's shoe laces with one of the strongest, most beautiful knots Dante had ever seen.

Dante: Thank you, Nathan. I see that you are admiring my brand new hat. Maybe you'd like one. At the pet store, they have different hats for every kind of pet. You can get one for a parrot or a hamster, or even a gecko.

Nathan: It is a very nice hat. But I don't like hats. Also, I do not have a pet.

Narrator 2: Nathan continued to stare at Dante's hat. He noticed the special changes. Dante had used the model glue to stick cut-up pieces of mango to the hat. There were little flies circling the mango pieces.
    Then a strange thing happened. A gecko attached to a kite string climbed out of Nathan's backpack. The gecko climbed up to Nathan's shoulder. Then he climbed onto Dante's shoulder. The gecko stared hungrily at the hat and the flies.

Dante: Who is this friend of yours, Nathan? Let me guess. You go to the bridge with this gecko. You lower him down with the kite string. He sticks to people's hats. That's how you steal the hats.

Nathan: Okay, all right, stop. You have got me! I took the hats. I admit it! I love hats.

Dante: I think your gecko is drooling on my shoulder.

Nathan: He loves flies, almost as much as I love hats.

Narrator 2: Nathan gave all the hats back. He promised to never steal again.

Narrator 1: When Dante got home, he asked to do some extra chores. He wanted to earn back all the money he had spent on the mango, the glue, and the hat. It was worth it, because he had solved another case.

The Case of the Kickball King

Characters

Narrator 1
Narrator 2
Kevin, the
  kickball king
Kayla, the pitcher
Zach
Andrew, captain of
  the rival team
Polly,
  the playground
  private eye
Ryan, Polly's
  sidekick

Narrator 1: Kevin had never been good at sports. When a game started, he always tried to find something else to do.

Narrator 2: Kevin had always hated kickball the most. But all that changed about a week ago. Suddenly, he turned into this amazing player. He wanted to play kickball constantly. Nobody could kick a ball higher or further. It was quite mysterious.

Kevin: C'mon, Kayla. Pitch the ball in here. Roll it fast, roll it slow, roll it any way you like. It makes no difference to me. I'm planning to kick this ball so far it will take a month for you to run it down.

Kayla: Here it comes.

Narrator 1: Kayla rolled the ball to Kevin. He kicked it really hard.

Kayla: There it goes!

Zach: It's still going. There's no chance I can catch it. That ball is way over my head. I can't believe it.

Narrator 2: The ball flew a long way. It rolled even farther, all the way to the edge of the blacktop. It was a homer, and three people scored. The Tigers grabbed the lead over the Sharks, 3–0. The next time Kevin came up, everyone backed way up.

Kevin: Pitch it to me again, Kayla. Roll it smooth, roll it bouncy, roll it any way you like. It makes no difference to me. I'm planning to kick this ball so far that you'll have to climb into a rocket and fly to the moon to get it back.

Kayla: See what you can do with this pitch.

Narrator 1: Kayla did her best trick pitch. She put some spin on the ball. But Kevin still kicked it hard.

Kayla: Wow. I see what you can do with that pitch.

Zach: I see it, too, barely! It's so high and so far that I can never catch it. I think I'll stand here and watch.

Narrator 2: It was another homer. Now the Tigers were winning, 4–0. This time the ball went completely over the school. Nobody had ever kicked a ball that far. The ball bounced across the street and finally came to rest on somebody's front lawn. A dog came bounding out and pawed at the ball.

Kevin: Too bad that pooch isn't one of your outfielders. You need him desperately. I am the kickball king!

Andrew: I'm not so sure. Until last week, you could barely even kick a ball. Now you're kicking it completely over the school.

Kevin: What exactly are you saying, Andrew?

Andrew: I'm saying that I'm suspicious. As captain of the Sharks, it's my duty to get to the bottom of this. I'm going to talk to Polly, the playground private eye.

Narrator 1: Andrew went and found Polly. She was sitting under a tree. She was talking to her best friend, Ryan. Andrew explained the situation.

Polly: How very interesting. Last week, Kevin could hardly kick the ball. This week, he's launching it completely over the school. That certainly is curious.

Ryan: What do you think we should do?

Polly: I suspect that Kevin has placed something hard in the toe of his shoe. That's what is giving him the extra kicking power. Ryan, do you remember who sits near Kevin in class?

Ryan: I remember that Zach's desk is right in front of Kevin's.

Polly: Perfect. We'll ask Zach to squeeze Kevin's toe. I'll bet Kevin doesn't feel a thing. Then we'll have proof. Then we'll know he has something stuffed into the toe of his shoe.

Narrator 2: Back in class, Zach waited for just the right moment. Then he turned around and squeezed Kevin's toe really hard. But Kevin's reaction was very strange and unexpected.

Kevin: Spin back around and face the front, Zach. What do you think you're doing?

Zach: Um . . . I am squeezing your toe. I want to be a shoe salesman when I grow up.

Kevin: Obviously! I mean, I feel it. Ouch! Oh, please quit. It aches. It stings. It burns. My toe is in agony.

Zach: I stopped squeezing your toe about five seconds ago.

Narrator 1: Zach told Polly about what had happened. The toe of Kevin's shoe felt very strange. It felt like it was full of little metal balls.

Narrator 2: But the weirdest thing: When Zach first started pinching him, Kevin didn't seem to notice. Only later did he start saying that it was hurting him. Then it seemed like Kevin was faking.

Polly: How very interesting. It certainly sounds like Kevin has something hidden in his shoe. But we still don't have any—pardon my pun— hard evidence.

Ryan: How can we get some? You always have lots of ideas, Polly.

Polly: I suspected this might happen, so I was prepared. Here's a magnet, Zach. Turn around and put this on Kevin's shoe. If it sticks, we'll have our proof. I'll wait for a few minutes, and then I'll walk over from my desk and check out the situation.

Narrator 1: Zach and Kevin were sitting at their desks. Zach turned around. He followed the plan.

Kevin: You keep turning around, Zach. Why are you so fidgety all of a sudden? It's really starting to irritate me. Hey, what did you just do?

Zach: Look. It sticks to your shoe.

Kevin: Why did you stick a magnet on my shoe?

Zach: It's just a little test. I might want to sell magnetic shoes when I grow up.

Kevin: Do you know what your test proved? It proved that you are a strange kid.

Polly: It also proved that you have something stuffed into the toe of your shoe. That's how you became king of the kickball universe all of a sudden.

Narrator 2: Kevin was finally cornered. He took off his shoe. He pulled out a sock full of little metal ball bearings. He was not the Kickball King. He was just a cheater. It was another case solved for Polly, the Playground Private Eye.

Kevin learned his lesson, too. He practiced and got better at kickball. He never kicked a ball completely over the school again. But with time, Kevin could kick a ball pretty far with his very own real right foot. Nobody ever kicked him around for being bad at kickball again.

The Big Sleuth-Off

Characters

Announcer
Narrator
Anna
Ziggy
Michael
Suspect 1
Suspect 2
Suspect 3

Announcer: Welcome to the Forensictown Sleuth-Off. Today, we have three talented young detectives competing in our junior division. The first one to solve a pretend crime will be the winner.

Let's get started. First, it makes sense to visit the scene of this pretend crime. Perhaps our sleuths will be able to gather some clues.

Narrator: The pretend crime scene was a picnic table in the town park. Lying on the ground nearby was a picnic basket. The basket was lying upside down.

It had been ripped apart. Food was scattered everywhere.

Anna: Look at this huge mess. That picnic basket is broken. There's a tomato lying in the grass over here. There's a piece of bread lying in the grass over there. This looks like the work of a wild animal. I would guess that a bear did this.

Ziggy: No way. This has all the signs of an alien invasion. I read somewhere that it is hard to have a picnic in space because there is no gravity.

　Most likely, these aliens had been waiting for just the right opportunity. They saw earthlings enjoying a picnic. They landed their spaceship in the park and raided all the food.

Michael: Hmmm. That is an interesting idea. I cannot help noticing this empty bag of chips. It is all crushed. But there are no crumbs inside.

　I think a person ate the chips first. Then they crushed up the bag. That person wants to make it look like an animal did this.

Announcer: Okay, junior sleuths. It is time for the second part of our competition. This is called the footprint event.

Narrator: The three detectives walked around the crime scene. They were looking for footprints that might offer clues.

Anna: Look, right there in the grass. Those marks were left by some very big feet. I knew it! If I had to guess I would say these are the footprints of a bear.

Ziggy: Wait a minute. Forget about space aliens. Look at those teeny footprints. I'll bet those belong to some kind of bird.

　Now it's all becoming clear. Someone trained a bird to swoop down on the picnic. It snatched up some sandwiches and chips and carried them back to its owner.

Michael: Hmmm. Another interesting idea. But I think those big tracks that Anna saw are a better clue.

Now, I have looked at the tracks very closely. If they were made by an animal such as a bear, I think there would be four different feet. Probably the front feet would be smaller than the back feet.

But I only see the same two feet over and over.

Anna: Maybe the bear was standing up when it walked.

Michael: Maybe. I think it is more likely that a person made those prints hoping to trick us. The person wants us to believe that a bear ate this food.

Announcer: All right, contestants. It is time for the third event in our competition. Please get out your magnifying glasses.

Narrator: The three detectives got down on their hands and knees. They used their magnifying glasses to hunt for the smallest clues.

Anna: I just found a piece of hair. It is long and brown. It does not look at all like a person's hair. I think it belongs to a bear.

Ziggy: Aha! I just found a small battery. This is the most important clue yet. Forget my theory that this crime was done by a trained bird.

That battery is crucial new evidence. I'm going to have to rethink everything. Think, Ziggy, think! Ouch! I think my brain is starting to overheat.

Michael: Hmmm. Do us all a favor, Ziggy. Do not think too hard. We do not want your ears to catch fire.

I just took a look at that hair Anna found. She is right. It is not a person's hair. But it does not belong to a bear either. The hair is fake. I bet it is part of a pretend bear costume that somebody made.

I still think someone is trying to play a trick. That person wants us to believe that a bear is on the loose.

Announcer: Are you ready, junior sleuths? It's time for the final part of the contest. Let's head over to the police station. We have rounded up three pretend suspects for this crime.

They will each offer an alibi. That means the suspects will try to prove that they were somewhere else when the crime took place.

Narrator: The three suspects were lined up against a wall. Each was a tough-looking character. They took turns giving their alibis.

Suspect 1: I work for the circus. My job is training bears.

    I also live right across from the park. I saw a family having a picnic. Then I decided to watch some television. My favorite show was on. I never miss it. So I could not have done this.

Suspect 2: I have an airtight alibi. I don't even live in Forensictown. I live 100 miles away in Hawker Heights. Do you think I hopped aboard an airplane and flew all the way here just to steal some picnic food? This is ridiculous.

Suspect 3: I did not do this. I was at my job. My job is sewing clothes. I work by myself in a small store downtown. There is no way that I would leave my job to steal picnic food.

Announcer: So there you have it, sleuths. You have heard from three suspects with three different alibis. Who do you think committed the crime? Think hard. Remember, the junior sleuth championship is at stake.

Anna: I think number one did it. You work for the circus. I think you used a trained bear to scare off the family. Then you came in and ate all the food that was left.

Ziggy: I'm absolutely 100 percent certain that suspect number two did this crime. You asked us whether you could have flown all the way from Hawker Heights.

    Oh, I think you did! I think you flew using a battery-powered jet engine. When you landed, you approached the picnic on stilts with bird-shaped feet on the bottom. That way everyone would think a bird raided this picnic.

    But it was you. You! It is all so clear.

Michael: Nice tries, Anna and Ziggy. It was number three. You work by yourself in a small store. So no one would notice if you were gone.

You work sewing clothes. It would be easy for you to sew a bear costume. As I have always said, I think you dressed as a bear to trick everybody. But I was not tricked. You did it. I am sure.

Announcer: Congratulations, Michael. You have been very logical. And you have solved the crime. You are the winner of the Forensictown Sleuth-Off. Here is your trophy.

Narrator: Suddenly, there was a popping sound. Suspect number two was standing on a pair of stilts with bird feet on the bottom. The suspect pushed a button and a battery-powered jet engine roared to life.

Suspect number two flew up into the air and hovered right above Michael. Then he snatched the trophy and flew off.

Ziggy: I knew it! I knew it!

Rabbits for Sale

Characters

Narrator 1
Narrator 2
Anthony, a boy
  selling pet rabbits
Taylor, a pet-
  rabbit buyer
Chris, a pet-
  rabbit buyer
Manny, a pet-
  rabbit buyer
TV pitch person
Pat, a toy
  store clerk

Narrator 1: Anthony's pet rabbit had ten babies. He had already sold seven of them to kids in his neighborhood. He was charging $2 for each rabbit. Anthony had three left to sell.

Narrator 2: As a bunny salesman, Anthony was an incredible smooth talker. He made all kinds of outrageous claims about what the rabbits could do. Anthony was so convincing that people could not help but believe him.

Anthony: Step right up. I have only three amazing bunnies left. Check out this little one with the gray spots.

Taylor: That looks like a nice rabbit. How much does it cost?

Anthony: For a limited time, I am offering this rabbit for the low price of $2. That is quite a deal. Please understand that this is a rare Norwegian Show Rabbit. It has already learned a number of commands, such as roll over and beg.

Taylor: I would love to have that rabbit. It will make a great pet. Here is $2.

Narrator 1: Taylor took the rabbit home. Taylor had a cage for it. But first the rabbit got to hop around the backyard. Taylor tried out the commands that Anthony had suggested.

Taylor: Okay, bunny. Beg. Can you stand up and beg? Here is a nice, tasty carrot. How about roll over. Can you roll over, bunny?

Narrator 2: Taylor tried all different commands in all different voices. The bunny just hopped around its pen. It was a nice pet, but it sure wasn't a rare Norwegian Show Rabbit. Meanwhile, smooth-talking Anthony had two rabbits left. He was determined to sell them.

Anthony: Listen up! I have only two incredible bunnies left. Take a gander at this little one with the spot covering its left eye.

Chris: I like the way that rabbit looks. It seems nice and friendly. How much money does it cost?

Anthony: Well, right now I'm pleased to extend a special offer. I'm asking $2. This isn't just any old rabbit, you see? This is an exotic Siberian Stunt Rabbit. This is an amazing creature. It can jump through hoops. It can even stand on its head.

Chris: This rabbit will make a very nice pet. I will take it. Let me give you $2.

Narrator 1: Chris brought the rabbit home. Chris had a cage for it to stay in. But first the rabbit got to hop around the backyard for a while. Chris tried to get it to do some tricks.

Chris: Will you jump through this hoop, bunny? I have a piece of lettuce just for you. Can you stand on your head? You can do it, bunny!

Narrator 2: Chris spent hours trying to get the rabbit to do tricks. It simply hopped around and wriggled its wet little nose. It made a great pet, but it sure wasn't an exotic Siberian Stunt Rabbit.

Now, Anthony the super salesman had just one rabbit left. He was determined to sell it.

Anthony: Gather 'round, everyone. I'm down to my very last rabbit. Take a look at this little one. It's completely white with no spots whatsoever.

Manny: Wow, a pure white rabbit! That is really cool looking. How much are you asking?

Anthony: This is my very last rabbit. As it happens, this is a one-of-a-kind. You can search the whole world over and you won't find another like this one. That's why I'm asking $2.

This is a unique Merlin's Magic Rabbit. It is the ideal magician's assistant. Simply place this rabbit in a black top hat. Say the magic word and it will disappear. Of course, the rabbit won't really disappear. It is simply an extremely well-trained creature that knows tricks that make it seem like it has disappeared. Then say another magic word and the rabbit will come back.

Manny: I can't believe it. I'm totally into magic. I know a bunch of incredible tricks. But I've always wanted a magic rabbit. Here, take my $2 and hand me that rabbit before someone else comes and snaps it up.

Narrator 1: Manny took the rabbit to his home. He carried it up to his room. Manny put the rabbit in his black hat. Then he tried to make it disappear.

Manny: Are you ready, rabbit! Abracadabra! Abracazam! I have a tasty slice of apple just for you. C'mon rabbit. Please disappear. Presto! Change-o! Scram!

Narrator 2: Manny tried every magic word he could think of. But the rabbit wouldn't disappear. Instead, it curled up in Manny's black top hat and went to sleep. It was going to be a very good pet, but it simply wasn't a unique Merlin's Magic Rabbit.

Meanwhile, Anthony had sold all ten rabbits for $2 each. Now he had $20 burning a hole in his pocket. He was trying to think of what to buy. Anthony turned on the television and saw an ad.

TV pitch person: Amaze your friends! Shock your parents! Stun your brothers and sisters!

Be the first one on your block to own a genuine Walk 'n' See Robot. It responds to spoken commands such as *walk, speed up, go left,* and *turn around.* It can climb steps and navigate mud puddles.

This incredible robot also has a built-in vision camera. That's right! You see what the robot sees. Simply tune your handheld monitor to 3-D vision or X-ray vision. It even comes with a built-in MP3 player and electric can opener.

Walk 'n' See Robot! It's brand new from Crank-O Toys. Just $19.99. But hurry. These robots are going fast.

Narrator 1: Anthony thought it sounded like a great toy. The price was right. He had made $20 by selling the rabbits. Anthony ran all the way to the toy store.

Anthony: Hey, I just saw an ad on TV for a Walk 'n' See Robot? Do you have any? Have they come in yet? They sound so cool. I want to make it roll through a mud puddle. I want to be able to look right through stuff with the X-ray vision. Then I'll switch over to 3-D vision.

Pat: Catch your breath, kid. Yes, we have that toy. I have one right here.

Anthony: Here's $20. I've got to get one of these right now. This is going to be the most stupendously cool toy ever!

Narrator 2: Anthony brought home his Walk 'n' See Robot. He inserted 12 batteries, just like it said in the instructions. He turned the robot on and put the built-in vision camera on the X-ray setting. Then he switched on the handheld monitor. He got nothing but static! Then he tried the 3-D setting. He still got only static. The robot did have flashing red lights, and it rolled around. It would be a pretty fun toy, but it certainly wasn't what he expected when he spent his money.

First, Anthony had tricked everyone else with the rabbits. Then, he got tricked himself. But he learned his lesson. Even though Anthony would always be a smooth talker, from now on, when he talked smoothly, he would also talk honestly.

The Pizza Power Hour

Characters

Narrator
Pepperoni
Mushroom
Olive
Alex
Alex's mom
Butch, the bully
Mia Fabulosi,
   a movie star

Narrator: Alex was just about to take a big bite of his favorite kind of pizza. Then he noticed something strange. His slice had exactly one piece of pepperoni, one mushroom, and one sliver of olive.

Then Alex noticed something even stranger. The pepperoni appeared to be smiling at him. Alex could swear he saw the olive wink.

Pepperoni: Hold on, pal. Not so fast. That's quite a set of choppers you have there. But I hope you'll use them to eat a hamburger or a taco.

Mushroom: I bet you are surprised. But please do not eat us. We are talking food. I do not think there are many other pieces of food in the world that are quite like us.

Olive: Olive here. Listen, I think we're pretty unique. I bet you've never encountered a talking slice of pizza. I'll bet we can be more useful to you uneaten than eaten.

Pepperoni: So here's the thing, buddy. You help us, and we'll help you. One hand washes the other, if you know what I mean.

So what is a problem that you are currently experiencing in your life? Sure, we may look like simple pizza ingredients. But we can offer you some very good advice.

Alex: Well, now that you mention it, I am having a problem with my parents. They just have so many chores for me. It's really boring, and it never ends.

As soon as I get one chore done, it's time to start on the next one. I want to play with my friends, not get stuck doing all these dull duties.

Mushroom: Here is what you do. Just say that you have done the work even if you have not. Pretend that it is finished. Your parents will not even be able to tell the difference.

Olive: Olive here. That is truly some good advice. I just want to second what Mushroom said. You can pretend that you are totally exhausted. That will make your act really convincing.

Narrator: Alex put the pizza slice in the refrigerator to keep it fresh. He wasn't so sure about the advice. Then again, it's not everyday that you meet talking food. He decided to give it a whirl.

Alex's mom: I asked you to clean up your room today. It is still a complete mess. There are clothes all over the floor.

Alex: I'm not sure if you can tell, but I did clean up my room. I did an extremely thorough job. Looks can be deceiving. My room may look messy. But I can assure you that this is a completely clean room.

Alex's mom: Okay then, Alex. I already paid you your allowance this week. It may not look like you have any money. But look closely. You will see that you do.

Stop this silliness, Alex. Go clean up your room right now!

Narrator: Alex could hardly tell his mom the truth. He had pretended to clean his room on the advice of a talking pizza slice. Alex went straight to the refrigerator. He planned to have a talk with that pizza.

Mushroom: So how did it go? Did our plan work?

Alex: No, it was a ridiculous idea. It didn't work in the least.

Pepperoni: Hey, simmer down. We give advice. We cannot guarantee results. We're counselors not magicians.

Now, why don't you let us redeem ourselves? What's another problem that you are having?

Alex: I guess I can give you guys a second chance. Okay, there's this kid down the block named Butch. He's always insulting me. I just got a new shirt that has a picture of this superhero called Ice Wind. He keep saying, "Nice Ice Wimp shirt."

Olive: Olive here. Here's exactly what you do. When he insults you, insult him right back. Maybe even up the ante. Say something worse or more hurtful just to show him that you are fierce and not to be messed with.

Mushroom: I think he is right. There is only one way to handle a bully. You have to be a worse bully.

Pepperoni: Ditto. This stuff is gold. I hope you realize we are giving you some good advice, buddy. Just make sure you follow it to the letter.

Why, I remember when I was a little pepperoni. This green pepper was giving me a rough time. Let's just say I offered a few choice criticisms. You should have seen that pepper's face. He may have been a green pepper. But by the time I was through with him, he looked like a red pepper.

Narrator: Alex put the pizza back in the refrigerator so it would stay fresh. He wasn't so sure about this new piece of advice, either. But maybe the talking food knew more about bullies than chores. He decided to give it a shot.

Butch: Hello, Alex. I see that you are wearing your Ice Wimp shirt today.

Alex: Who is your favorite superhero? Are you a big fan of the Fantastic Fool? I think maybe you like the Great Goofball. No wait. I know. I bet your very favorite superhero is the Boy Blunder.

Butch: Let's decorate your nice shirt.

Narrator: Butch took out a permanent marker. He wrote the words "Ice Wimp" in big letters on Alex's shirt. Butch thought that was very funny. He laughed and laughed.

By now, it was clear to Alex that the talking pizza slice gave terrible advice. It had gotten him in trouble twice. As soon as he got home, he opened up the refrigerator.

Mushroom: Did it work? Did you stick it to Butch? Did you show that boy who the boss is?

Alex: No. That was a preposterous plan. Butch was an even worse pest.

Pepperoni: Hold on, big guy. It sounds like you are trying to lay the blame on us.

We're just humble pizza fixings that give advice. That's where our job ends. We're not responsible if you fail to follow our advice properly.

Olive: Uh, Olive here. I sense that you're disappointed. You aren't planning to eat us are you? If you think our advice is bad, you should see how we taste. We've been sitting in that fridge for a week. I guarantee we'll give you indigestion.

Alex: Don't worry. I won't eat you. That would be a terrible waste of a talking pizza.

Fortunately, I've come up with a plan. I think the three of you should have your own television talk show. I'm sure millions of people would tune in to watch you. And since I'll be your agent, I'm sure I can make more money than I'm getting for my allowance.

Narrator: And that is how *The Pizza Power Hour* came to be. The very first guest on the show was the movie star, Mia Fabulosi.

Mushroom: I am glad you are here to talk about your new movie. It sounds like it is really good. Tell us about it.

Mia Fabulosi: My new movie is called *Spring*. It is about a man and woman who meet. They fall in love.

Pepperoni: Hold on a moment. This sounds like one of those mushy flicks. Personally, I prefer a good action picture with fast cars and rocket ships.

Olive: Olive here. I'm so honored that you are our guest tonight. Ms. Fabulosi . . . Mia . . . I have to say that I am one of your biggest fans. Have you every considered doing a movie in which you star opposite an olive?

Narrator: *The Pizza Power Hour* became a big hit. Pepperoni, Olive, and Mushroom became very famous. And as Alex expected, he became extremely rich as their agent.

However, the talking trio couldn't help themselves! During commercial breaks, they still loved to dish out bad advice to members of the studio audience.

Mushroom: Who wants to be spoiled with rotten advice from talking pizza?

Narrator: People came from all around to visit the show. Even Butch came. They all hoped to hear the latest bad advice.

Mushroom: Eat gooey chocolate cake right before going to the dentist.

Olive: Leave your umbrella at home if it is cloudy outside.

Pepperoni: Here is my favorite advice. Always talk with food in your mouth!

Narrator: After three seasons, people realized that it was a bad idea to get bad advice from pizza, and they moved on to the next big thing. The show was cancelled and Alex vowed never to eat pizza again.

Gwen, the Cranky Sorceress

Characters

Narrator 1
Narrator 2
Glendella,
  Gwen's mother
Gwen
Magic Creature 1
Magic Creature 2
Magic Creature 3
Magic Creature 4

Narrator 1: Perhaps you have never heard the tale of Gwen, the Cranky Sorceress. It goes something like this. Once upon a time, there was a young sorceress named Gwen. She was extremely irritable.

Narrator 2: People did not like her much. That made her lonely. Gwen had heard about a magic spell that could make a new friend. Her mother warned her that the spell was hard to say.

Glendella: You must be careful, dear. I do not know if you are ready. You are young and you have not done much magic yet.

    This is a very hard spell. If you say it wrong, who knows what will happen.

Gwen: I don't care, Mom. It's your fault that I don't have any friends. Why do I have to be cooped up in this stupid castle? You always ruin everything for me.

I'm going to say the spell. There's nothing you can do about it.

Narrator 1: It really was a difficult spell, just as Glendella had warned. You had to say the following words exactly:

Bippito Alpsoweed Nickowack Splend
Didem Yo Item Pop Mako Me Friend

Gwen stormed out of the castle and walked across a meadow. Soon she saw something to turn into a friend.

Gwen: Look here. I've found a daisy. When you look closely, a daisy is kind of an ugly flower. I don't really like the color yellow. But daisies are prettier than violets and roses. Those are flowers I really hate.

When I say the spell, I hope this flower will turn into a decent friend. At the very least, I hope it will be someone I can tolerate. Well, here goes:

Bippito Alpsoweed Nickowatt Splend
Didem Yo Item Pop Mako Me Friend

Narrator 2: Bam! Just like that, the flower turned into something very strange.

Gwen: I must not have used the proper words for the spell. What in the world are you?

Magic Creature 1: Check out my red nose! Look at this big bump on my back! Can you guess what I am?

I am a camel clown. I like to do funny pranks and tell jokes. I can also go a long time without drinking water.

Gwen: It looks like I messed up the spell. I'll just have to say it again correctly. I'll turn you into someone I can be friends with.

Bippito Alpsoweed Nickowack Splend
Didem Yo Item Pop Maky Me Friend

Narrator 1: Kabam! The camel clown was gone in a poof of smoke, only to be replaced by a new creature.

Gwen: Now what? I must have really goofed up the spell this time. You are even weirder than that camel clown.

Magic Creature 2: I'm pretty unusual, right? My name is Zorat. I'm a belamund. Some people say I look like a snake made out of a row of basketballs.

   I can slither and bounce at the same time. That's pretty cool, don't you think?

Gwen: Actually, it is not cool at all. I'm really not looking for any slithery, bouncy friends right now. Now if you'll excuse me, I am going to try the spell again and try to get it right this time:

Bippilo Alpsoweed Nickowack Splend
Didem Yo Item Pop Mako Me Friend

Narrator 2: Boom! The creature that looked like a long row of balls disappeared. A new one showed up in its place.

Gwen: Now what?! You would think that this magic trick wouldn't be so strict. I mess up one word of the spell and a creature like you appears. What are you anyway?

Magic Creature 3: I am a mud puppet. I cannot do too much by myself. Come over here and pick me up. Slip me onto your hand. Be careful. You will get mud all over your hand and arm.

   I can make all kinds of funny faces. I can talk in silly voices. We will have lots of fun together.

Gwen: I cannot imagine having any fun with you.

Magic Creature 3: I can also read minds. I know what you are thinking. Please do not send me back. I think we could be friends.

Gwen: This is a nightmare. I am having the worst luck. I just want to find a decent friend. I have to get this spell right:

Bippito Alpsoweed Nickowack Splend
Ditem Yo Item Pop Mako Me Friend

Narrator 1: Kaboom! There was a bright white flash and the mud puppet was gone.

    Yet another new strange creature appeared in its place. Hey, it was a difficult spell. Get one word wrong, miss one little letter even, and it changed everything.

Gwen: Oh no! I cannot take this anymore. Let me guess. You are a hideous square monster.

Magic Creature 4: Ha-ha. Close. Actually, I am a very rare breed of dog. As you can see, my shape is a perfect cube. Maybe you wanted a cute dog. I'm a cube dog. I have eyes and ears and a mouth. I am covered in thick pink fur.

    Of course, I don't have feet or a tail. How do I move, you might wonder? I simply start vibrating. I can actually move very quickly that way. I can even fetch a ball. I can also bark in five different languages. I can't roll over, because I have no curves. But I can flip over onto another of my flat sides.

Gwen: Obviously, you are very talented. But you are also a big cube dog. I've had just about enough of this. I just want a normal friend. I'm going to say the magic words and send you on your way.

Magic Creature 4: Oh, I will say the magic words. That's one of my five different languages!

Bippito Alpsoweed Nickowack Splend
Didem Yo Item Pop Mako Me Friend

Narrator 2: Bang! Just like that, Gwen turned into a big pink cube dog. Now she finally had the perfect friend she had been looking for.

    The change was good for Gwen. As a dog, she was not so cranky. As a dog, she was much nicer. (She also stopped doing magic spells.) The two cube dogs lived happily ever after.

Reading Level Key

Level 1 = 2.0–3.9   Level 2 = 4.0–5.9

Cliffhangers

Can the Thrilling Three Save Grandville?

Level 1: Narrator 2, Flexor, Rocket, Match-Head
Level 2: Narrator 1, X-Spec, the Bungler, Questioner

Will Erin Win the Third Annual Willow Grove French Fry Eating Contest?

Level 1: Narrator 2, Alice-Nicole, Crowd, Questioner
Level 2: Narrator 1, Announcer, Erin, James

Will Isabella's Time Machine Work?

Level 1: Chris, Sailor 2, Cave person 1, Questioner
Level 2: Narrator, Isabella, Sailor 1, Cave person 2

Spooky Stuff

There's Always an Explanation

Level 1: Narrator 1, Mrs. Blackmore, Spooky voice, Suit of armor
Level 2: Narrator 2, Mr. Blackmore, Liz, Thornton Blackmore

A Ghost at the Gifford School

Level 1: Narrator 2, Cody, Laura, Aaron
Level 2: Narrator 1, Juan, Michelle, Mrs. Fletcher

A People Story

Level 1: Narrator 1, Ick, Blap, Driffle
Level 2: Narrator 2, Grog, Trigor, Snink

Mysteries

The Case of the Disappearing Hats

Level 1: Steph, Narrator 2, Shopkeeper 1, Nathan
Level 2: Narrator 1, Dante, Shopkeeper 2, Shopkeeper 3

The Case of the Kickball King

Level 1: Narrator 1, Kayla, Zach, Ryan
Level 2: Narrator 2, Kevin, Andrew, Polly

The Big Sleuth-Off

Level 1: Anna, Michael, Suspect 1, Suspect 3
Level 2: Announcer, Narrator, Ziggy, Suspect 2

Just for Laughs

Rabbits for Sale

Level 1: Narrator 1, Taylor, Chris, Pat
Level 2: Narrator 2, Anthony, Manny, TV pitch person

The Pizza Power Hour

Level 1: Mushroom, Alex's mom, Butch, Mia Fabulosi
Level 2: Narrator, Pepperoni, Olive, Alex

Gwen, the Cranky Sorceress

Level 1: Narrator 2, Glendella, Magic Creature 1, Magic Creature 3
Level 2: Narrator 1, Gwen, Magic Creature 2, Magic Creature 4